This journal belongs to

CHERISHED MOMENTS

Before Your Birth Day...

A Pregnancy Journal
© 2009 Ellie Claire Gift & Paper Corp.
www.ellieclaire.com

Compiled by Barbara Farmer
Designed by Lisa and Jeff Franke for Ellie Claire, Minneapolis, MN

Scripture references are from the following sources: The Holy Bible, New International Version® NIV®. © 1973, 1978, 1984 by International Bible Society. Used by permission of Zondervan. The New King James Version (NKJV). Copyright © 1982 by Thomas Nelson, Inc. Used by permission. The Holy Bible, New Living Translation® (NLT). Copyright © 1996, 2004. Used by permission of Tyndale House Publishers, Inc., Wheaton, Illinois. *The Message* © 1993, 1994, 1995, 1996, 2000, 2001, 2002. Used by permission of NavPress Publishing Group. The New Century Version® (NCV). Copyright © 1987, 1988, 1991 by Thomas Nelson, Inc. Used by permission. The Living Bible (TLB) copyright © 1971. Used by permission of Tyndale House Publishers, Inc., Carol Stream, Illinois 60188. All rights reserved.

Excluding Scripture verses and poetry, references to men and masculine pronouns
have been replaced with gender-neutral references.

ISBN 978-1-934770-56-6

Printed in China

Before Your

Birth Day...

a pregnancy journal

Congratulations!

The bond between mother and child begins at the first hint
of life within. Even more so when the tests are confirmed.
The rush of love, the heart filling with joy, and even the
queasy stomach—all memories to ponder deep inside.

Preserve the awesome experience of your pregnancy in
the whimsical pages of *Before Your Birth Day*. Write a letter
to your child, record blessings to bestow upon Baby, and
capture the emotions and wonders that are a part of the
amazing development of your little one from conception
to birth. Cherish all these wonderful events as a keepsake
for you and your child to enjoy in the years to come.

May God bless your new little one.

To Baby,

....

....

....

....

....

....

....

....

....

....

....

....

....

....

....

....

....

Love Mommy

To Baby,

Love Daddy

*W*here did you come from, baby dear?
Out of the everywhere into the here...
How did [it] all just come to be you?
God thought about me, and so I grew.
But how did you come to us, you dear?
God thought about you, and so I am here.

George MacDonald

My body is the knitting machine for this miracle. How can that be?
There's no conscious effort to focus my thoughts on my tummy to
develop cells and organs and extend the spinal chord and eyelashes.
Wow.... *I* am fearfully and wonderfully made as well as my baby!

*Y*ou made all the delicate, inner parts of my body and knit me together
in my mother's womb. Thank You for making me so wonderfully complex!
Your workmanship is marvelous—and how well I know it.

PSALM 139:13-14 NLT

A mother's joy begins when new life is stirring inside...when a tiny heartbeat is heard for the very first time and a playful kick reminds her that she is never alone.

A time to reflect

It may be a bit early to feel a kick or hear a heartbeat, but you know there is a stirring in your soul. What was it that made you wonder? When did you first sense the need to inquire and how long did you keep it to yourself?

....

....

....

....

....

....

....

....

....

....

....

Every good action and every perfect gift is from God.
These good gifts come down from the Creator of the sun, moon,
and stars, who does not change like their shifting shadows.

JAMES 1:17 NCV

There is an enduring tenderness in the love of a mother to a child that transcends all other affections of the heart.

Washington Irving

A prayer from the heart

Dear Heavenly Father, How overwhelming is the feeling I have toward
this life within me. How amazed I am at the connection we already have.
Please lead me through this journey and gently keep my baby
cradled in Your care. Amen.

Love each other with genuine affection,
and take delight in honoring each other.
ROMANS 12:10 NLT

Babies are living jewels,
dropped unstained from heaven.

Sir Frederick Pollock

A poem for Baby

A little face to look at,
A little face to kiss;
Is there anything, I wonder,
That's half so sweet as this?

Don't you see that children are God's best gift?
The fruit of the womb His generous legacy?
PSALM 127:3 THE MESSAGE

A grand adventure is about to begin.

Winnie the Pooh

A tip for Mommy

A great way to start on this road to motherhood is to prepare and pamper
yourself. Help your body thrive with rest, nutrition, and exercise.
Feed your heart, mind, and soul with words of wisdom and good advice.
And enjoy the perk of special attention from others.

I will pour out My Spirit...and My blessing on your children.
They will thrive like watered grass, like willows on a riverbank.
ISAIAH 44:3-4 NLT

Babies come into our earth to bring us
a fresh breath of heaven.

A thought to inspire

The blessing of an earthly family gives us only a hazy picture
of the blessing in God's heavenly family.

Janette Oke

Your love, O Lord, reaches to the heavens,
Your faithfulness to the skies.

PSALM 36:5 NIV

When, for the first time,
I saw your little face—time changed.
It would never again be counted
by the tick of a clock,
but measured instead
by the beat of your heart.

A time to reflect

Love children especially...they live to soften and purify our hearts.

Fyodor Dostoyevsky

....

....

....

....

....

....

....

....

....

....

....

....

How natural it is that I should feel as I do about you,
for you have a very special place in my heart.

PHILIPPIANS 1:7 TLB

Making a decision to have a child—
it's momentous. It is to decide forever to have your
heart go walking around outside your body.

Elizabeth Stone

A prayer from the heart

Lord, this little one is a part of me, safe and warm and close inside my
tummy, and even though the umbilical cord is severed at birth,
that connection is not. Are we not attached to You in the same way?
No matter the space, time, or circumstances, we are never more than
a heartbeat away from Your love. Thank You for that. Amen

This is the way you shall bless the children...: "The Lord bless you and
keep you; The Lord make His face shine upon you, and be gracious to you;
the Lord lift up His countenance upon you, and give you peace."

NUMBERS 6:23-26 NKJV

We never know the love of the parent till
we have become parents ourselves.

Henry Ward Beecher

A poem for Baby

This little tiny baby
Was sent from God above
To fill our hearts with happiness
And touch our lives with love
He must have known we'd give our all
And always do our best
To give our precious baby love
And be grateful and so blessed.

Everyone who believes that Jesus is the Christ is God's child, and whoever
loves the Father also loves the Father's children.

1 JOHN 5:1 NCV

However time or circumstance may come between a mother and her child, their lives are interwoven forever.

Pam Brown

A thought to inspire

Your child will never grow too old to hear you say "I love you."

Jan Dargatz

---

*Be of one mind, live in peace. And the God of love
and peace will be with you.*

2 CORINTHIANS 13:11 NIV

God sends children to enlarge our hearts; and to make us unselfish and full of kindly sympathies and affections.

Mary Howitt

A time to reflect

Babies change the ordinary to the extraordinary;
they change a house into a home.

O God, remember us and bless us....
And let God bless all who fear God—
bless the small, bless the great.

PSALM 115:12-13 THE MESSAGE

Higher than every painter, higher than every sculptor and than all artists do I regard the one who is skilled in the art of forming the soul of children.

John Chrysostom

A prayer from the heart

Dear Heavenly Father, How can I not marvel at the creation of life.
You have placed a soul of infinite worth into my womb—a special place
You made to sustain this little life—how incredible! Amen.

....

....

....

....

....

....

....

....

....

....

....

The Lord who created you...the one who formed you says,
"...I have called you by name; you are Mine.

ISAIAH 43:1 NLT

In a world where everyone seems to be larger and louder than yourself, it is very comforting to have a small, quiet companion.

Peter Gray

A tip for Mommy

Preparing a nursery, buying the necessities, doctor visits, parenting classes;
so much to do, so little time. But paying attention to your little one
now is as important as when the baby arrives in your arms. Find time
daily to sit down and place your hands on your belly. Actually hold
your little one and let your baby feel your attentive affection.

The Lord is my shepherd, I shall not be in want. He makes me lie down in
green pastures, He leads me beside quiet waters, He restores my soul.
PSALM 23:1-3 NIV

Jesus loves me! This I know,
For the Bible tells me so.
Little ones to Him belong;
They are weak, but He is strong.

Anna B. Warner

Remember how simple it was as a child to know the love of God?
The good news is, God's love is still the same.

·····

We have known and believed the love that God has for us. God is love, and he
who abides in love abides in God, and God in him.

In every child is planted the seed
of a great future.

A time to reflect

A baby is a rose with all its sweetest leaves yet folded.

....

....

....

....

....

....

....

....

....

....

....

....

For I know the plans I have for you," declares the Lord, "plans to prosper you and not to harm you, plans to give you hope and a future."

JEREMIAH 29:11 NIV

We do but borrow children of God
and lend them to the world.

John Donne

A prayer from the heart

This baby is a part of me now and needs me in every respect;
but in a while, an individual person with personality and plans
and purpose will emerge. Lord, give me Your compassion and
understanding to let my child be who You intended.

As a father has compassion on his children, so the Lord
has compassion on those who fear Him.

PSALM 103:13 NIV

A mother holds her children's hands
for a while, their hearts forever.

Jewish Proverb

A blessing for Baby

When you were small and just a touch away,
I covered you with blankets against the cool night air.
But now that you are tall and out of reach,
I fold my hands and cover you with prayer.

Dana Maddux Cooper

Your statutes are my heritage forever; they are the joy of my heart.
PSALM 119:111 NIV

A young child, a fresh, uncluttered mind,
a world before him—to what treasures will you lead him?

Gladys M. Hunt

A thought to inspire

Take time to notice all the usually unnoticed, simple things in life.
Delight in the never-ending hope that's available every day!

Let our sons in their youth grow like plants. Let our daughters
be like the decorated stones in the Temple.

PSALM 144:12 NCV

God invented parenthood. He is for us. He is for each of our children. He is champion of their lives, their years, their health, their calling, and their eternal destiny.

Ralph T. Mattson and Thom Black

A time to reflect

What God is to the world, parents are to their children.

Philo Judaeus

....

....

....

....

....

....

....

....

....

....

....

....

I am the Lord your God, and I have set you apart from
other people and made you My own.

LEVITICUS 20:24 NCV

God's interest in the human race is nowhere better evinced than in obstetrics.

Martin H. Fischer

A prayer from the heart

Lord, this creation of Yours, how amazing! I've seen sunsets and butterflies and thunderstorms and more, but this little person growing inside of me surpasses all of those. My body is knitting together a masterpiece. Thank you for allowing me to be a part of creating another human soul. Amen.

For by Him all things were created: things in heaven and on earth...
all things were created by Him and for Him.

COLOSSIANS 1:16 NIV

The simplest and commonest truth seems new and wonderful when we experience it the first time in our own life.

Marie von Ebner-Eschenbach

A tip for Mommy

It isn't the great big pleasures that count the most;
it's making a great deal out of the little ones.

Jean Webster

....

....

....

....

....

....

....

....

....

....

....

....

From the very first day you heard and recognized the truth of what
God is doing, you've been hungry for more.

COLOSSIANS 1:6 THE MESSAGE

Who is queen of baby land?
Mother kind and sweet,
And her love, born above,
Guides the little feet.

A thought to inspire

Mother is the name we call the one who held us so close and
warm when the world was so new and cold. She fed us, clothed us,
took care of our needs. What a lovely portrait of God's care.

....

....

....

....

....

....

....

....

....

....

....

....

I will give the land to your little ones—your innocent children.
DEUTERONOMY 1:39 NLT

Every child born into the world is a new thought of God, an ever-fresh and radiant possibility.

Kate Douglas Wiggin

A time to reflect

Children are not poets.
They are too busy being poems.

O Lord, You alone are my hope. I've trusted You, O Lord, from childhood.

Thank You for this precious child—
The sleepy eyes, the gummy smile,
The wrinkly hands and wiggly feet—
Keep them happy, pure, and sweet.

A prayer from the heart

Thank You, Father God, for giving me the gift of motherhood;
letting me witness and experience a newly created life.
Thank You for showing me Your inexhaustible love by giving me
the opportunity to love the same way. Amen.

May the God of your fathers, the Almighty, bless you with
blessings of heaven above and of the earth beneath.

GENESIS 49:25 TLB

I wish for you a curiosity that leads you from one wonderful moment to another, and a contentment to be happy wherever you may be.

A poem for Baby

Wynken, Blynken and Nod one night
Sailed off in a wooden shoe—
Sailed on a river of crystal light
Into a sea of dew.

Eugene Field

How joyful are those who fear the Lord.... Their children will be successful
everywhere; an entire generation of godly people will be blessed.

PSALM 112:1-2 NLT

Underneath all my other thoughts of the day I wonder, who is this person growing and turning inside of me. And does Baby wonder about me?

A thought to inspire

You are a little less than angels, crown of creation, image of God.
Each person is a revelation, a transfiguration,
a waiting for Him to manifest Himself.

Edward Farrell

What a wildly wonderful world, God! You made it all, with Wisdom at
Your side, made earth overflow with Your wonderful creations.

PSALM 104:24 THE MESSAGE

Running errands and talking on the phone,
I am pleasantly reminded that I am not alone....
I look forward to your birth,
when I can kiss your skin,
but for now I will just smile,
As I feel you play within.

Was that a kick? Hmm...could be, or it could be the peanut butter
and pepper sandwich I had for lunch. Oh, I can't wait to see those
fingers and toes, watch them flicker and quiver while Baby sleeps
and be reminded of the tickle and joy they once produced inside me.

....

....

....

....

....

....

....

....

....

....

....

Always give thanks to God the Father for everything.
EPHESIANS 5:20 NCV

It will be gone before you know it. The fingerprints on the wall appear higher and higher. Then suddenly they disappear.

Dorothy Evslin

A prayer from the heart

Dear Lord, these past few months have gone buy so quickly and I know
my due date will arrive in like fashion, so help me to take the time to
cherish each new day. If I can practice that now, I will better recognize future
special moments and pause to enjoy them as they should be enjoyed. Amen.

These are the children God has given me. God has been good to me.
GENESIS 33:5 NCV

It is true that you may occasionally overhear
a mother say
"Children must have their naps, it's mother who knows best."
When what she really means by that is that she needs a rest.

Donna Evleth

A tip for Mommy

The advice to sleep when the baby does is easier said than done.
However, it is a worthwhile habit to start as it leads to so many benefits.
When you are refreshed, normal baby activities—feeding, diapering,
bathing, entertaining—become so much more enjoyable for both of you.

He Himself gives life and breath to everything,
and He satisfies every need.

ACTS 17:25 NLT

Little tiny hands, a precious rounded knee
pushing and twisting that no one can see.
Oh sweet child kicking up your heels,
it is our little secret that only I can feel.

Children help us rediscover the joy, excitement,
and mystery of the world we live in.

Just as you'll never understand the mystery of life forming in a pregnant
woman, so you'll never understand the mystery at work in all that God does.

ECCLESIASTES 11:5 THE MESSAGE

Loving a child is a circular business...
the more you give, the more you get,
the more you get, the more you want to give.

Penelope Leach

It is not how many things you provide for your children that counts.
It is how much you give of yourself.

Give, and it will be given to you. A good measure, pressed down,
shaken together and running over, will be poured into your lap.
For with the measure you use, it will be measured to you.

LUKE 6:38 NIV

Little baby on the way, getting bigger every day,
Kicking mommy here and there; God please listen to our prayer.
Keep our baby safe and strong, let his time with us be long,
Help us teach him right form wrong, and we shall praise Thee all day long.

Tina Greenfield

A prayer from the heart

Lord, help me to trust You, knowing You are ever mindful of me and my child—
my whole family. Not only do You watch over us, but Your angels surround us at
Your command with power to guide, protect, and comfort. Thank You. Amen.

He has put His angels in charge of you to
watch over you wherever you go.

PSALM 91:11 NCV

To be a child is to know the joy of living.
To have a child is to know the beauty of life.

A poem for Baby

Two tiny feet that wave in the air,
Two tiny hands that tug at your hair,
Cute bottom for patting, adorable face;
A bundle of joy to love and embrace.

Why is everyone hungry for *more*? "More, more," they say. "More, more."
I have God's more-than-enough, more joy in one ordinary day.

PSALM 4:6-7 THE MESSAGE

All the things in this world are gifts and signs of God's love to us. The whole world is a love letter from God.

Peter Kreeft

A thought to inspire

For all the precious gifts of life
The best must surely be
A baby who brings added joy
Into a family.

....

....

....

....

....

....

....

....

....

....

....

I'll bless you—oh, how I'll bless you! And I'll make sure that your children flourish—like stars in the sky! like sand on the beaches!

GENESIS 22:17 THE MESSAGE

Precious baby you come to me
from where love is infinite
where angels speak a language
only babies understand.

Aida Gandini

A time to reflect

There is nothing more thrilling in this world, I think, than having a child that is yours, and yet is mysteriously a stranger.

Agatha Christie

....

....

....

....

....

....

....

....

....

....

....

....

I prayed for this child, and the Lord answered
my prayer and gave him to me.

1 SAMUEL 1:27 NCV

$\mathcal{B}$abies come wrapped in all our hopes and dreams—but we have to loosen the wrappings to give them space to grow.

Phyllis Hobe

You will be with my baby, Lord, guiding and protecting.
You said so. I'm holding to Your Word. I have read of all
the promises that You have kept and my confidence
only grows. Thank You for being trustworthy. Amen.

I am with you, and will protect you wherever you go....
I will be with you constantly.
GENESIS 28:15 TLB

One hundred years from now it will not matter what my bank account was, how big my house was, or what kind of car I drove. But the world may be different, because I was important in the life of a child.

Forest Witcraft

A poem for Baby

Women know the way to rear up children (to be just);
They know a simple, merry, tender knack
Of tying sashes, fitting baby-shoes,
And stringing pretty words that make no sense,
And kissing full sense into empty words.

Elizabeth Barrett Browning

My dear, dear friends, if God loved us like this, we certainly ought to love each other. No one has seen God, ever. But if we love one another, God dwells deeply within us, and His love becomes complete in us—perfect love!

1 JOHN 4:11-12 THE MESSAGE

My sweet baby, to hold you in my womb, to cradle you in my arms, to cherish you in my heart always—there is no other greater joy.

There are many ways of holding a baby—swaddled tight, cuddled
under the chin, facing out to see the world. What a tender and loving
means by which to discover aspects of your child's demeanor
while at the same time holding your baby close to your heart.

*F*rom His abundance we have all received one
gracious blessing after another.
JOHN 1:16 NLT

Just as there comes a warm sunbeam into
every cottage window, so comes a love—
born of God's care for every separate need.

Nathaniel Hawthorne

A time to reflect

God knows everything about us. And He cares about everything. Moreover,
He can manage every situation. And He loves us! Surely this is enough
to open the wellsprings of joy.... And joy is always a source of strength.

Hannah Whitall Smith

....

....

....

....

....

....

....

....

....

....

....

....

All your children shall be taught by the Lord,
and great shall be the peace of your children.

ISAIAH 54:13 NKJV

When the first baby laughed for the first time the laugh broke into a thousand pieces and they all went skipping about.

Sir James M. Barrie

Teach me, Father, to value each day,
to live, to love, to laugh, to play.

Kathi Mills

I'm bursting with God-news! I'm walking on air.
I'm laughing.... I'm dancing my salvation.

1 SAMUEL 2:1 THE MESSAGE

Mothers...are the first book read, and the last put aside in every child's library.

C. Lenox Redmond

A tip for Mommy

If you haven't started already, talk to your Baby, say a prayer or a blessing
out loud for your baby to hear. Developing ears are eager to listen.

Our children will live in Your presence.
And their children will remain with You.

PSALM 102:28 NCV

Pregnant women!...they had that preciousness which they imposed wherever they went, compelling attention, constantly reminding you that they carried the future inside, its contours already drawn, but veiled, private, an inner secret.

Ruth Morgan

While your body is expanding and changing and revealing symptoms of
pregnancy no one has ever told you about, consider the beauty there is:
the glow of your checks, the twinkle in you eye, the way it is so easy to rest
your hand on your belly for comfort. What a lovely picture of love.

....

....

....

....

....

....

....

....

....

....

....

....

*Your beauty should come from within you—
the beauty of a gentle and quiet spirit.*
1 PETER 3:4 NCV

Who will you look like, how will you be?
Will you look like Daddy or me?
Ten little fingers and ten little toes,
A wrinkled up forehead and a cute button nose.
You will be crying with that first cold touch,
And so will I because I love you so much.

Wendy Dahlke

What shall I wish for you baby? Health or wealth untold,
Or the courage to face new challenges, the strength to be brave and bold?
But whatever I wish for you, baby, I hope this lesson you'll learn,
The greatest of all God's blessings is to love and be loved in return.

....

....

....

....

....

....

....

....

....

....

....

Then Jesus took the children in His arms,
put His hands on them, and blessed them.

MARK 10:16 NCV

There are many things that we get from our children, including love and meaning and purpose and an opportunity to give. They help us to maintain our sense of humor.

James Dobson

Dear Lord, I know there will be so many emotions accompanying
parenthood, but may the undercurrent of every situation
hold an element of pure joy. Amen.

---

*O*ur mouths were filled with laughter, our tongues with songs of joy....
The Lord has done great things for us, and we are filled with joy.

PSALM 126:2-3 NIV

In pregnancy, there are two bodies, one inside the other. Two people live under one skin.... When so much of life is dedicated to maintaining our integrity as distinct beings, this bodily tandem is an uncanny fact.

Joan Raphael-Leff

A poem for Baby

Feel my pulse,
Know my heart,
You, dear child,
Life impart.

────────────────────────────

Your wife shall be like a fruitful vine in the very heart of your house,
your children like olive plants all around your table.

PSALM 128:3 NKJV

I love these little people; and it is not a slight
thing when they, who are so fresh from God, love us.

Charles Dickens

Straight from heaven! Baby, you are an elaborate creation of God that can only be described as angelic. You cling to me and I am filled with awe.

This is my prayer for you: that your love will grow more and more; that you will have knowledge and understanding with your love.

PHILIPPIANS 1:9 NCV

*he God who made your children will hear your petitions. He has promised to do so. After all, He loves them more than you do.

James Dobson

How can anyone love my child more than I do? My heart bursts with adoration for this little one. But God's love does go deeper, and higher, and wider. It is perfect and all-consuming and just what my baby needs.

Therefore know that the Lord your God, He is God, the faithful God who keeps covenant and mercy for a thousand generations with those who love Him and keep His commandments.

DEUTERONOMY 7:9 NKJV

A babe in the house is a wellspring of pleasure,
a resting place for innocence on earth,
a link between angels and man.

Martin Farquhar Tupper

A poem for Baby

"Cuddle and love me, cuddle and love me,"
Crows the mouth of [rosey] pink:
Oh the bald head, and oh the sweet lips,
And oh the sleepy eyes that wink!

Christina Rossetti

I will be a Father to you, and you shall be My sons and daughters,
says the Lord Almighty.

2 CORINTHIANS 6:18 NKJV

You may have tangible wealth untold;
Caskets of jewels and coffers of gold.
Richer than I you can never be—
I had a mother who read to me.

Strickland Gillilan

The sound of your voice is music to Baby's ears. Enjoy a little time each day reading to your child from children's books or your own favorite books. Do you remember the nursery rhymes from your childhood? Pass on well-loved poems and stories during these tender moments.

....

....

....

....

....

....

....

....

....

....

....

....

....

My child, if your heart is wise, my own heart will rejoice!

PROVERBS 23:15 NLT

Dear Little One,
You bring sunshine to my life. You give me hope
for the future. You make me see the whole world
from a new and wonderful point of view.

A thought to inspire

Your eyes are forming and blinking and winking, Baby, but really
what do you see? Even though I have seen so much more, your presence
has opened my eyes to a whole new perspective on life.

When I was a child, I spoke as a child, I understood as a child,
I thought as a child.

1 CORINTHIANS 13:11 NKJV

My child, you hold the whole of my heart in your small hands.

A time to reflect

The first handshake in life is the greatest of all:
the clasp of an infant fist around a parent's finger.

Mark Beltaire

....

....

....

....

....

....

....

....

....

....

....

I've cultivated a quiet heart. Like a baby content in its
mother's arms, my soul is a baby content.

PSALM 131:2 THE MESSAGE

Just to be is a blessing.
Just to live is holy.

Abraham Heschel

A prayer from the heart

Thank You, Father God, for life; for more than just existence,
for meaning and purpose. Thank You for the experience of
bringing this little life into the world. Amen.

With Your unfailing love You lead the people You have redeemed.
In Your might, You guide them to Your sacred home.

EXODUS 15:13 NLT

Precious one,
So small, so sweet
Dancing in on angel feet.
Straight from Heaven's
brightest star
What a miracle you are!

A blessing for Baby

May your tiny feet always carry the stardust of Heaven
as you journey through life here on Earth. God be with you
and bless you, my precious little one.

Surprise us with love at daybreak; then we'll skip
and dance all the day long.

PSALM 90:14 THE MESSAGE

All things bright and beautiful,
All creatures great and small,
All things wise and wonderful,
The Lord God made them all.

Cecil Frances Alexander

Seeing the world through the eyes of a child is like entering
the Land of Oz. The everyday black-and-white workaday world
becomes a vivid and colorful landscape of animated life.

O Lord, You are my God; I will exalt You and praise Your name,
for in perfect faithfulness You have done marvelous things,
things planned long ago.

ISAIAH 25:1 NIV

There is no other closeness in human life like the closeness between a mother and her baby—chronologically, physically, and spiritually they are just a few heartbeats away from being the same person.

Susan Cheever

A time to reflect

As content as babies are when snuggled in their mother's arms,
so God wants us, His children, to feel when nestled close to Him.

....

....

....

....

....

....

....

....

....

....

....

....

*How great is the love the Father has lavished on us, that we should
be called children of God! And that is what we are!*

1 JOHN 3:1 NIV

I am yours, you are mine.
Of this we are certain.
You are lodged in my heart, the small key is lost.
You must stay there forever.

Frau Ava

A prayer from the heart

Dear Lord, Thank You for sending this child to me so that I may experience a love so deep and true. I know this is only a reflection of the love You have for me and I am overwhelmed. May my baby come to know this same amazing love that comes from You. Amen.

I say to myself, "The Lord is mine, so I hope in Him."

LAMENTATIONS 3:24 NCV

The potential possibilities of any child are the
most intriguing and stimulating in all creation.

Ray L. Wilbur

A tip for Mommy

God created your baby to fulfill a specific purpose. Ask God to help
you be keenly aware of the special abilities and gifts your child possesses.
Then actively encourage your child in the way he or she should go.

The Lord will fulfill His purpose for me;
Your love, O Lord, endures forever.

PSALM 138:8 NIV

In bringing up children, what good mothers and fathers instinctively feel like doing for their babies is usually best after all.

Benjamin Spock

The most important thing she'd learned over the years was that there was no way to be a perfect mother and a million ways to be a good one.

Jill Churchill

Even though you are bad, you know how to give good gifts
to your children. How much more your heavenly Father
will give good things to those who ask Him!

MATTHEW 7:11 NCV

Before you were conceived I wanted you
Before you were born I loved you
Before you were here an hour I would die for you
This is the miracle of Mother's Love.

Maureen Hawkins

A time to reflect

There's only one pretty child in the world, and every mother has it.

The Lord says, "As surely as I live, your children will be
like jewels that a bride wears proudly."

ISAIAH 49:18 NCV

Feeling fat lasts [for] nine months but the joy of becoming a mom lasts forever.

Nikki Dalton

Lord, help me during the next little while, to get me through the
uncomfortableness, the tiredness, the waiting, and let me see the big picture:
I am bearing a child, one who bears the image of You. Amen.

Love is patient and kind.... It always trusts,
always hopes, and always endures.

1 CORINTHIANS 13:4, 7 NCV

Life is always a rich and steady time when you are waiting for something to happen or to hatch.

E. B. White

A poem for Baby

Cleaning and scrubbing can wait 'til tomorrow,
For babies grow up, we've learned to our sorrow...
So quiet down, cobwebs, dust, go to sleep...
I'm rocking my baby, and babies don't keep.

For the Lord is always good. He is always loving and kind, and His
faithfulness goes on and on to each succeeding generation.

PSALM 100:5 TLB

Of all the joys that lighten suffering on earth,
what joy is welcomed like a newborn child?

C. Newton

A thought to inspire

No other experience of receiving compares to the one where our arms
open up and welcome in the life of our son or daughter.

When a woman gives birth, she has a hard time, there's no getting around it.
But when the baby is born, there is joy in the birth.

JOHN 16:21 THE MESSAGE

A baby can turn your life upside-down and make it feel right side-up. A baby can turn your world around and take it in a wonderful new direction.

Phyllis Hobe

A time to reflect

A baby will make love stronger, days shorter, nights longer,
bankroll smaller, home happier, clothes shabbier, the past forgotten,
and the future worth living for.

He gathers the lambs in His arms and carries
them close to His heart.

This little one, though not yet here,
Is loved so much, has grown quite dear.
Delivery time is growing near,
That's why we pray our plea You'll hear.
Please help us Lord, we pray to Thee
With thankful heart, on bended knee.

Tina Greenfield

Dear Heavenly Father, I ask You now for Your strength and
protection during the delivery of my baby. May I trust You completely
to hold me and my child in Your loving hands. Amen.

The Lord is faithful and will give you strength and will protect you.

2 THESSALONIANS 3:3 NCV

I've never known such an all consuming love as I felt the minute this child was born. What absolute joy! What amazing beauty!

A poem for Baby

What shall we wrap the baby in?
Nothing that fingers have woven will do:
Looms of the heart weave love ever new:
Love, only love, is the right thread to spin,
Love we must wrap the baby in!

*K*now that you yourself are a miracle.

Norman Vincent Peale

A thought to inspire

You, dear mother of this child, are special and loved
by the One who created you.

_____

_____

_____

_____

_____

_____

_____

_____

_____

_____

_____

_____

God saw all that He had made, and it was very good.
GENESIS 1:31 NIV

You are the poem I dreamed of writing
the masterpiece I longed to paint.
You are the shining star I reached for
In my ever hopeful quest....
You are my child.
Now with all things I am blessed.

A time to reflect

There are two requirements for our proper enjoyment of every earthly blessing which God bestows on us—a thankful reflection on the goodness of the Giver and a deep sense of the unworthiness of the receiver. The first would make us grateful, the second humble.

Hannah More

You have chosen to bless my family. Let it continue before You always. Lord, You have blessed my family, so it will always be blessed.

1 CHRONICLES 17:27 NCV

After the baby was born, I remember thinking that no one had ever told me how much I would love my child.

Nora Ephron

A prayer from the heart

It is indescribable, Lord, the love that has welled up in my heart.
May I always see this wonderful little child as a divine blessing,
to me as well as to the world. Amen.

May the Lord richly bless both you and your children.
PSALM 115:14 NLT

As you begin your life, precious child of mine, I wish for you friends, health, laughter, justice, kindness, patience, and much more.

A blessing for Baby

I wish you love, and strength, and faith, and wisdom,
Goods, gold enough to help some needy one.
I wish you songs, but also blessed silence,
And God's sweet peace when every day is done.

Dorothy Nell McDonald

The fruit of the Spirit is love, joy, peace, patience, kindness,
goodness, faithfulness, gentleness and self-control.

GALATIANS 5:22-23 NIV

When you were born my world screeched to a halt. It ceased to exist. Now it is *our* world.

Worlds can be found by a child and an adult bending
down and looking together under the grass stems or
at the skittering crabs in a tidal pool.

Mary Catherine Bateson

Those who fear the Lord are secure;
He will be a refuge for their children.

PROVERBS 14:26 NLT

A new baby is like the beginning of all things—
wonder, hope, a dream of possibilities.

Eda J. LeShan

A time to reflect

If our children are blank pages upon which we write their future,
then we must carefully consider what we want to write.

Patricia H. Rushford

A newborn opens a door from God
and lets grace pour in.

A prayer from the heart

Lord, it's an awesome job, this parenting thing. Give me the grace,
goodness, and determination I need to do the best possible job....
It's up to You and me, Lord. Be with me every step of the way. Amen.

Patricia Lorenz

The Lord your God is with you.... He will take delight in you, He will
quiet you with His love; He will rejoice over you with singing.

ZEPHANIAH 3:17 NIV

The most wonderful sound our ears can hear is the sound of a newborn baby.

A tip for Mommy

A baby learns quickly that crying communicates. The mother's job is
then to be an interpreter of the cries. Is Baby hungry, wet, cold, hurt, or in
need of a cuddle? Say a little prayer for discernment; the Lord is there to help.

Jesus said, "Let the children come to Me.... For the Kingdom
of Heaven belongs to those who are like these children."

MATTHEW 19:14 NLT

The difficult thing about children is that they come with no instructions. You pretty well have to assemble them on your own.

James Dobson

What is the most important aspect of being a parent? Is it the right equipment for the nursery? The appropriate apparel for every occasion? The latest advice from the experts? Or is it the loving presence of a parent?

The Lord is my strength and my shield; my heart trusts in Him, and I am helped. My heart leaps for joy and I will give thanks to Him in song.

PSALM 28:7 NIV

My babe so beautiful! It thrills my heart with tender gladness just to look at you.

A poem for Baby

God has blessed us.
He chose us to receive the gift of you.
And I believe, with my whole heart
He gave us to you so you might grow
in patience, too.

*You're beautiful with God's beauty, beautiful inside and out!
God be with you.*

LUKE 1:28 THE MESSAGE

In the sheltered simplicity of the first days after
a baby is born, one sees again the magical closed circle.
The miraculous sense of two people existing only for each other.

Anne Morrow Lindbergh

A prayer from the heart

Heavenly Father, thank You for the privilege of having children.
Allow every day...to be a special experience. Help me to savor
every moment that comes, and may my children always be confident
in my love and devotion to them. Amen.

Kim Boyce

May the Lord make your love increase and overflow for each other.

1 Thessalonians 3:12 NIV

And the Lord loved the baby, and sent congratulations and blessings.

2 SAMUEL 12:24-25 TLB